THE GOLD RUSH

Bobbie Kalman

 Crabtree Publishing Company
www.crabtreebooks.com

LIFE IN THE OLD WEST

Created by Bobbie Kalman

To little Chiara,
who enriches our lives

Author and Editor-in-Chief
Bobbie Kalman

Managing editor
Lynda Hale

Senior editor
April Fast

Project editor
Kate Calder

Researcher
Amelinda Berube

Copy editors
Hannelore Sotzek
Jane Lewis

Photo researcher
Kate Calder

Special thanks to
National Cowboy Hall of Fame;
Dawson City Museum and Historical Society

Computer design
Lynda Hale
Robert MacGregor (cover concept)
Campbell Creative Services

Production coordinator
Hannelore Sotzek

Separations and film
Dot 'n Line Image Inc.

Printer
Worzalla Publishing Company

Crabtree Publishing Company

www.crabtreebooks.com   1-800-387-7650

Cataloging-in-Publication Data
Kalman, Bobbie
    The gold rush
(Life in the Old West)
Includes index.
ISBN 0-7787-0079-8 (library bound) ISBN 0-7787-0111-5 (pbk.) This book describes how the
prospect of finding gold lured both men and women west and discusses how they lived, the
difficulties they faced, and the impact of the gold rush on the Native Americans.
1. North American—Gold discoveries—Juvenile literture. 2. Gold mines and mining—North
America—History—19th century—Juvenile literature. 3. Klondike River Valley (Yukon)—Gold
discoveries—Juvenile literature. 4. California—Gold discoveries—Juvenile literature. [1.
California—Gold discoveries. 2. Klondike River Valley (Yukon)—Gold discoveries. 3. Gold mines
and mining.] I. Title. II. Series: Kalman, Bobbie. Life in the Old West.
E46.K35 1999   j338.2'741'097 21   LC 99-11520
                                                                         CIP

**Published in
the United States**
PMB 16A
350 Fifth Ave.
Suite 3308
New York, NY
10118

**Published
in Canada**
616 Welland Ave.,
St. Catharines,
Ontario, Canada
L2M 5V6

**Published in the
United Kingdom**
73 Lime Walk
Headington
Oxford
0X3 7AD
United Kingdom

**Published
in Australia**
386 Mt. Alexander Rd.,
Ascot Vale (Melbourne)
V1C 3032

TABLE OF CONTENTS

4 Gold Strike

6 The Great Gold Rushes

8 Getting to the Gold Fields

10 Staking a Claim

12 How was Gold Found?

14 Tools of the Trade

16 Life at the Mines

18 Women and Children

20 Native Land

22 Boomtowns

24 Law and Order

26 Striking it Rich

28 A Dangerous Prospect

30 The End of the Gold Rushes

31 Glossary

32 Index & Acknowledgments

GOLD STRIKE

In the 1800s, most of the people in the United States and Canada lived in the eastern states and provinces. Communities, roads, and pastures marked the landscape. Eastern towns and cities were becoming crowded with newcomers from Europe and Britain. Land in the East was expensive. Many people wanted to have their own land and escape from the cramped conditions of city life.

The West

In the early 1800s, the western areas of the United States and Canada were mainly unsettled. Miles of grassy plains and steep mountains lay to the west of the busy, populated eastern cities. At first, only a small number of people made the long and difficult journey west. Most of them were men who went to start ranches or work as cowboys.

Gold beckons

In the mid-1800s, gold was discovered in the rivers of western North America. It took time for people to learn of this discovery. When the news of gold findings traveled east, many people did not believe these reports to be true. When some of the gold was brought to the East, however, people quickly became interested! Rumors and newspaper headlines convinced people that there really was gold in the West. People across the continent were eager to make a claim and become rich. Thousands of people made the trip west in search of their fortune. A great **migration** of people to the West in search of gold was known as a **gold rush**.

The prospectors

The people who headed west to search for gold were called **prospectors**. When they arrived, there were plenty of opportunities for them to become **miners**. Anyone who came to the gold fields had a chance of striking gold.

THE GREAT GOLD RUSHES

There were many gold rushes, and each brought people to different areas of the rugged, unsettled West. Some gold rushes brought thousands of people and lasted several years. In addition to miners, business people also came. They opened shops and offices in the busy towns that developed around the mines. The increase in businesses helped small towns grow into large cities. Other gold rushes lasted less than a year. The towns in those areas were abandoned after all the gold was taken.

(below) This unknown prospector is standing in front of Sutter's mill, which was built by James Marshall. James Marshall was the first newcomer to discover gold in the West, but unfortunately he never became rich.

The California gold rush

The first gold rush in the North American West was the California gold rush. In January of 1848, James Marshall was building a sawmill on the American River when something caught his attention. He found flakes of gold in the riverbed. News of his find traveled quickly and, by 1849, the California gold rush was under way. People from all over the world left their families and businesses to travel to California in search of gold. These prospectors were known as the "forty-niners." Due to this gold rush, California's population jumped from under 30,000 to more than 300,000 in just ten years!

Gold fever

Gradually, prospectors moved farther away from the California gold fields in search of more gold. Great amounts of gold and silver were soon discovered in Nevada. These precious metals are still mined in Nevada today. As some prospectors moved east to Nevada, others struck gold in the North between Oregon and British Columbia. In the 1890s, some Californian miners decided to return to the East after they could no longer find gold. Along the way they stopped in Colorado and struck gold there. Prospectors flocked to any place gold was found.

The Klondike gold rush

Another famous gold rush was the Klondike gold rush. The Klondike is a region of the Yukon territory in Canada and is near the Arctic. The Klondike gold rush began in 1896—almost fifty years after the California gold rush. Gold was found in mountainous and forested regions that had long, freezing winters. The precious nuggets were first discovered in a creek stemming from the Klondike River. The creek where this gold was found was known as Bonanza Creek. A bonanza is a rich source of precious metal. Ten million dollars worth of gold was mined in the Klondike during that gold rush!

*Some miners in the Klondike were known as **sourdoughs**. Sourdough is a type of bread that the miners ate. It was often the only food they had available in a mining camp or on the journey north to find gold. In the picture below, this sourdough in Dawson City is using a team of dogs to pull his equipment.*

Business people, farmers, and factory workers left their homes and families in the East to travel to the gold fields. Others came from distant countries. They packed their tools, clothing, and food and said goodbye to their friends. The travelers knew the journey would be dangerous, and they were not sure if they would ever return home.

On their own

Many prospectors left their loved ones behind. The journey through unknown territories would put women and children at risk. Some could not afford to pay the additional travel costs to take their family along. Other miners left family members at home to run their business in case they did not strike it rich.

The sea voyage

People who came from great distances to the gold fields traveled over land or by sea. Reaching the gold fields by sea was difficult. Large ships had expensive fares, and small boats were often cramped, dirty, and dangerous. An overseas trip could take from five weeks to seven months. When the boat finally arrived at the port, the travelers still had to make a long overland journey.

This map shows the land and sea routes used to reach the California and Klondike gold rushes. Which route looks the most difficult?

route to Klondike
route to California
routes to San Francisco
route to Alaska

There were two routes by sea from New York to San Francisco. The first went around South America. This journey took up to seven months. A faster sea journey let passengers off at Central America, where they traveled through the jungle and sailed up alligator-infested rivers to Panama City. From there, they boarded another ship and sailed to San Francisco.

Traveling by wagon train

The journey by land to California was often more difficult than the journey by sea. Some people traveled across the entire continent to reach the gold fields! These miners used covered wagons pulled by horses or mules to transport their belongings. They often traveled together in groups called **wagon trains**. Traveling in a group was safer than traveling alone. The miners were able to help one another find food or repair broken wagons. Each day, from sunrise to sunset, the wagon train would continue its journey with brief stops to eat and feed the animals.

Hazards of the overland trip

Some people traveled to the gold fields on foot and carried their possessions on their back. Whether by wagon or on foot, the overland journey was extremely dangerous. Travelers had to cross swift rivers and steep mountains in sweltering heat and freezing temperatures. There was little food to eat, and people often became ill. Many travelers died trying to get to the gold fields. A large number of gold seekers gave up and turned back before reaching the gold fields.

Difficult terrain

Determined travelers overcame obstacles such as rivers and steep inclines. They built **scows**, or rough boats, to cross lakes and rivers. In the Klondike, they had to carry supplies over steep, icy slopes and rugged landscapes. In later years, **tramways** powered by horses or steam engines also hauled heavy loads of goods and supplies up steep mountainsides. Tramway operators charged customers by the weight of their load.

(above) Thousands of settlers used covered wagons like this one to travel to the West. People often walked alongside the wagon and helped push its heavy load.

STAKING A CLAIM

When prospectors first arrived at a gold field, they began searching for gold wherever they could. When they found an area of unsettled land, they "claimed" it as their own by leaving their tools on the ground. The tools showed other prospectors that the spot was taken. As greater numbers of people began arriving at the gold fields, many prospectors began mining for gold on land that was being mined by someone else. To settle land disputes, miners set up rules so that each miner would have his or her own property on which to search for gold. Marking property was called **staking a claim**.

Claim regulations

When miners found an area suitable for mining, they marked their claim. Some hammered shovels or stakes into the ground. Others made piles of rocks or put up a sign with their name on it. Claims in popular areas, such as along rivers, could be as small as ten square feet (3 square meters). Claims that were farther away from the river could be more than fifty square feet (15 square meters). Abandoned claims could be taken by anyone. In some places, a claim had to be left for a week before it was considered abandoned. In others, a two-day waiting period was enough.

Registering claims

As more people arrived, the competition for land and gold became fierce. People tried to **claim jump**, or take over the claims of others. Eventually, prospectors had to register their claims at a **commissioner's office**. Having a registered claim provided proof of ownership and allowed miners to buy and sell their claims.

This woman in the Klondike is staking a claim by sticking a marker in a tree.

How was Gold Found?

Gold was found in the form of small flakes, nuggets, or dust. Some was scattered in the dirt and gravel at the bottom of riverbeds, and some was buried underground. The gold came from larger **deposits** that were buried deep in underground rock. These deposits are called **lodes** or **vein deposits** because they are spread throughout the narrow seams of the rock like veins in a leaf.

Golden streams

Over thousands of years, water from rivers and streams **eroded**, or washed away, hard rock. Gradually, particles of gold in the rock were loosened and carried away with the moving water. This gold, found in rivers, streams, and other areas just below the ground's surface, was called **placer gold**. Much of the placer gold was found in the bends of rivers and streams, where the current of the water slowed, and the gold settled at the bottom.

How did miners get the gold?

Gold is eight times heavier than sand and stones. Prospectors washed the gold in a lake or river to separate it from the dirt. When dirt containing gold was **washed**, the gold settled on the bottom of the pan. By swirling the pan around, the dirt mixed with the water. When the water was tipped out of the pan, the dirt poured out as well. The gold-laden dirt at the bottom of the pan was washed over and over again until nothing remained but the gold.

Teamwork

Prospectors often worked together on one claim to mine for gold. The job was much easier with five or six pairs of hands! Some prospectors learned how to mine for gold by trial and error, but it was much easier to learn from someone

with more experience. Experienced miners sometimes helped the new miners, who were called **greenhorns**. They showed greenhorns the best methods for finding gold.

Buried gold

In order to find buried gold, miners dug holes as deep as 100 feet (30 meters). A miner at the bottom of a deep hole put dirt and gravel into a bucket that was attached to a rope. The miners above ground pulled up the bucket. Then they washed the dirt hoping to see the gleam of gold.

The team of miners, shown above, is working together in the hopes of finding buried gold. The miner at the bottom is chipping away with a pick, and the men above him are washing the dirt in a sluice (see page 14).

TOOLS OF THE TRADE

When prospectors arrived at the gold fields, some had tools they brought from home. Many had no tools at all. Tools could be bought from small **tent stores** at the gold fields. Most prospectors, however, bought only a few necessary tools because they had little money and store-bought items were expensive.

The basic mining tools were a shovel (left), a pick (right), and a pan (below). A miner used the pick to break away or loosen pieces of rock. The shovel was needed for moving dirt and gravel to the location of the other mining equipment.

Prospectors separated the gold from dirt using a pan. Some miners panned all day long for gold. Others used the pan to test if there was gold in a certain area. When gold was found, the miners used larger equipment to separate the gold from the dirt and rock.

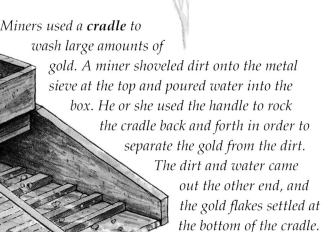

*Miners used a **cradle** to wash large amounts of gold. A miner shoveled dirt onto the metal sieve at the top and poured water into the box. He or she used the handle to rock the cradle back and forth in order to separate the gold from the dirt. The dirt and water came out the other end, and the gold flakes settled at the bottom of the cradle.*

Hydraulic mining

Hydraulic mining was a method used in the later years of gold mining, after most of the placer deposits had been taken. It enabled miners to get gold located deep in hard rock deposits. Large **flumes**, or channels, directed water from a dammed stream to the mining site. A metal pipe attached to the end of the flume sent out a high-pressure spray of water. The spray from the pipe was strong enough to blast away rock and soil. The runoff water carrying dirt and gravel was directed into sluices, where the gold was separated.

Sluices were also used to wash gold. A sluice was a long wooden trough through which water could flow. Dirt was shoveled into the sluice, where running water washed over it. The gold sank to the sluice bottom, where it was caught by wooden **riffles**, or ridges. Large sluices called **long toms** could wash dirt at the same rate as two or three people using pans.

LIFE AT THE MINES

The California gold rush attracted people from all over the world. Hopeful prospectors from Britain, Europe, Australia, China, Portugal, and Mexico flooded into San Francisco in 1849, when gold was discovered there.

(above) Prospectors often had their portraits taken to send home to their families. Some posed holding mining tools. (opposite page bottom) This large group of miners took a break from a long day of mining to pose for a photograph.

(above) Many African American people who were brought to the gold fields as slaves were able to find enough gold to buy their freedom.

(right) These American and Chinese miners are working together, but many Chinese miners were treated badly by other miners, who harmed them or destroyed their property. Their claims were highly taxed because they were not Americans.

(above) This little "miner" is ready for the gold fields. Do you think she became a miner when she grew up?

(top right) These two women made a lot of money but not on the gold fields. They sold food to hungry miners in the Klondike.

(middle) The life of a miner was often lonely. Many prospectors spent their spare time doing chores such as scrubbing dirty laundry.

Although many women remained in the East, some chose to make the challenging journey to the gold fields. Some traveled with their husbands. Other adventurers were single women excited about new opportunities that the West had to offer.

Married women

Married women grew vegetables, cooked meals, mended clothes, and looked after the children. Some worked with their husband mining gold. Families had an advantage over single miners. A prospector and his wife could each have a claim, giving the family twice as much land to mine. Many married women took jobs in a nearby town if their husband could not find gold.

Going alone

Without a family to care for, a single woman had more time to take on different jobs. She could hire herself out as a laundry washer or cook. A single woman could work as a singer or waitress at a hotel or saloon. She could also make money by selling baked goods or renting out cots to travelers. The money a single woman earned was entirely her own, and she could spend it as she desired. These women, however, were often treated poorly. Only the most determined succeeded.

This woman is bringing lunch to her husband and his teammates. They work hard and need plenty of food.

Children of the gold rush

Children also worked hard to help the family. They helped with chores in the home and did as much as they could to find gold on the claim. Some children earned money as errand runners, newspaper carriers, and assistants at stores and hotels. Some searched for spilt gold dust in saloons. Only a few children were lucky enough to attend school.

Time for play

Children in the West had much more free time than those in the East. Girls spent time outside rather than staying indoors learning how to cook and sew. Although western children did not have as many toys as those in the East, they had fun in other ways. They learned to play musical instruments and played games such as Snap the Whip and Wolf Over the River.

When there were enough children in an area, a one-room school was set up. Children whose parents did not need them to help on the claim went to school as soon as they were old enough to attend.

Before the gold rushes began, the land that held gold in its rivers and hills was home to Native Americans. They fished in the rivers and lived off the land. Some moved from place to place in search of buffalo, which provided them with food, shelter, and clothing.

Hurting a way of life

When gold was discovered in California, thousands of prospectors arrived on Native American lands. The prospectors were more concerned with finding gold than ensuring they were not harming the way of life of the Native Americans. Miners dammed rivers, cutting off water supplies to Native American villages. They polluted the waters, killing wildlife as a result. Settlers killed thousands of buffalo for their skins. Thousands more buffalo were shot for sport. Settlers also brought diseases that caused thousands of Native Americans to die.

Forced to change

Without enough animals to hunt for food, the Native Americans were soon starving. They began fighting with the miners over land. The government offered the Native Americans areas of land called **reservations** and promised to give them food as well as materials for making clothes and building homes. Native Americans were eventually forced to abandon their way of life.

The real cost of gold

Some prospectors kidnapped Native American children and sold them to others or forced them to work on mining claims. Native Americans died from diseases, starvation, and in battle. In total, more than 120,000 Native Americans died during the California gold rush.

Prospectors in the Klondike often paid Native people to help carry their equipment to the gold fields.

BOOMTOWNS

As thousands of people moved to the West, settlements began forming quickly. Within days, unsettled areas became busy towns. A town was likely to appear anywhere prospectors were mining. These new towns were called **boomtowns**. A boomtown is a town where the population grows quickly, or booms.

Boomtown homes

The first buildings in a boomtown were rough shacks that were built to provide the miners with shelter. When people began making enough money, they built more comfortable places to live and work. A gold-rush town often had well-built, two-story structures as well as rough and dirty camps.

Busy roads

Boomtowns were busy places. People hurried through the streets on foot, on horseback, and in wagons or carriages. The roads were made of packed dirt that turned into deep, sticky mud when it rained. Instead of concrete sidewalks, gold-rush towns had wooden boardwalks.

Boomtown Business

In addition to prospectors, merchants and other business people moved to a boomtown in order to set up stores, hotels, restaurants, and saloons. Businesses made money selling goods and services to the miners. The success of these businesses attracted more people to the town.

Going to town

Many prospectors lived outside the towns but went into town for supplies, entertainment, and news. In a boomtown there were plenty of jobs for unsuccessful miners. They worked in stores, hotels, and restaurants. Some even abandoned the gold mines and stayed in town to make money running a business.

Long visits

During warm weather, the miners worked hard on their claims, but in the winter many moved into town. In the Klondike, most of the miners remained in town for the entire winter. Winter on their claim was long, cold, and extremely lonely. Creeks and rivers became frozen or too cold to pan. Miners could not dig into the frozen ground. It was much easier to spend the season in a place where there were jobs and people.

(above) The people of Dawson City are gathered around a rare sight—a hot air balloon.
(bottom) To get mail from home, the prospectors in San Francisco waited for hours in line at the post office.

LAW AND ORDER

Crime was a major problem in the mining camps. There were few police, and the miners of the West were far from the cities and courts of the East. Many people with criminal records moved west to get away from the law. Greed and competition led to theft and murder on the claim sites. Many people tried to steal land and gold from others. In the mining camps, drinking and gambling often resulted in fights in which miners were seriously injured or even killed.

Vigilante justice

Without enough police to control crime, miners started making their own laws and justice systems. They did not contact police and often carried out their own idea of punishment for people who committed crimes. People who enforced their own laws are known as **vigilantes**. Vigilante laws were harsh and often added to, rather than prevented, the chaos and lawlessness of the California gold rush.

Harsh punishment

A person accused of committing a crime in a mining camp was usually arrested and punished immediately and without a fair trail. A person found guilty was often ordered by the vigilantes to leave the area and never return. Harsher punishments included **flogging**, scarring a person's face with a hot branding iron, cutting off ears, or hanging.

Rules and regulations

The government in the Klondike learned a lesson from the lawlessness of the California gold rush. Police forces were more effective in the Klondike than they had been in California.

They always got their man!

Canadians were prepared to handle the type of crime that got out of control in the South. A sourdough was not allowed to enter the Yukon without at least a year's worth of supplies. This law reduced theft and also helped prevent death by starvation and malnutrition. The Klondike was still a wild place with its share of gambling, drinking, fighting and stealing, but the North West Mounted Police helped keep crime under control.

*Canadian police officers were called **Mounties** because they policed the North mounted on horseback. This Mountie is taking away liquor from whiskey smugglers.*

When miners struck gold, they often built their family a large Victorian-style house on the outskirts of a boomtown. Living in a fancy home made them feel wealthy and civilized, like their friends back east. People liked to show off their newfound wealth. Building a large house was a good way to show off!

Have you ever heard someone talk about "hitting pay dirt?" This expression comes from the gold rush. To prospectors, pay dirt, was dirt that had the glitter of gold in it. Nowadays, pay dirt means discovering something useful or profitable.

Millionaires of the gold rush

Not everyone found their fortune, but a few miners made over a million dollars by digging on one small claim! Prospectors were not the only ones who could make a fortune, however. Landowners made huge profits selling land to eager settlers. Many business people earned a lot of money by operating businesses such as stores, hotels, and law firms.

Grubstaking

Many prospectors spent all their money in traveling to the gold fields. They did not have enough left over to buy mining equipment. Often, wealthy miners or townspeople loaned them a **grubstake**. A grubstake was a supply of equipment, food, or money that allowed the prospector to get started. In return, the miner had to promise to give the lender of the supplies a share of the profits. Giving money to a person or business in return for a share of the profits is also known as **investing**.

Wasted money

Few miners struck it rich, and even fewer managed to stay rich. Some successful miners spent all their money on clothing, travel, and liquor. Many lost their riches at the gambling tables, as shown in the picture on the right. Others invested their money in promising businesses. Unfortunately, the companies they supported often went out of business, and the investors lost their money as a result.

(above) Not everything that glittered was gold. Prospectors had to keep from being fooled by **fool's gold**. Fool's gold was a hard substance called **iron pyrite** that looked like gold but was not valuable. Fool's gold shattered when it was hammered, and it felt gritty. True gold, however, could be hammered thin and was smooth to the touch.

These miners hiking up the Chilkoot Pass on the way to the Klondike risked losing their footing and falling to the bottom of the huge incline. Avalanches also made traveling through snowy mountain ranges dangerous.

The prospectors who rushed to the West were often not prepared for the rugged landscape of the western frontier. Most of the people who dreamed of finding gold had never been exposed to the harsh conditions of the West. They seldom knew of what to expect. Endless chores, dangerous crossings, bad weather, sickness, and the death of friends cooled the gold fever of some travelers. They were shocked at the crime and greed involved in the search for gold.

Crossing the rugged landscape

Just getting to the gold fields was dangerous. Navigating wagons through steep, narrow passes in the mountains was difficult and often deadly. A wagon could tip over or roll down a steep mountainside. Prospectors also had to cross fast-flowing rivers. Many drowned trying to cross rivers in narrow canoes or poorly-made rafts.

Freezing cold

Miners worked long hours in all kinds of conditions—sometimes standing up to their waist in freezing water. Being in cold water for hours often caused people to get **rheumatism**, a disease that caused swelling and stiffness in muscles and joints.

Dirty towns and camps

Towns and camps were unsanitary and did not have proper sewers or clean water. This unclean environment often caused people to become ill or infected with diseases. People rarely had nutritious meals because of scarce food supplies and became sick as a result of malnutrition. Diseases and malnutrition caused many deaths.

(above) Losing a loved-one was not unusual in a mining town or camp. Mining incidents such as falling into the deep holes dug in search of gold took the lives of many miners.

Sometimes hungry bears stumbled across a claim or mining camp. Bears lived throughout the western wilderness, from California to the Klondike.

THE END OF THE GOLD RUSHES

Eventually, the supply of gold began to run out. To get at the gold that remained, big equipment such as **dredges** were needed. Dredges were huge machines powered by an engine that scooped gravel from deep rivers and lakes. Only large companies could afford such expensive equipment. Individual miners found that they could no longer mine on their own and went to work for large companies. Company miners worked for wages. Any gold that they mined went to the company and not to them. There were no more overnight millionaires! The rush of people slowed and then stopped altogether. Eventually, people began to pack up and leave.

Effects of the gold rushes

The gold rushes played an important role in North American history. The discovery of gold caused people to make journeys to faraway places such as California and the Klondike. In the process of searching for gold, roads were built and buildings were constructed. Newcomers from other countries became part of North America's multicultural heritage. Thousands of people stayed in the West and started new lives. The Native Americans, however, lost their way of life. In California, ex-miners turned to farming the fertile Sacramento Valley. Cities such as Sacramento and San Francisco continue to grow and thrive.

The California gold rush brought thousands of settlers west, causing towns like San Francisco to grow into huge cities.

Ghost towns

Some towns continued to thrive without gold, but others were abandoned forever. Abandoned towns are known as **ghost towns**. Some ghost towns still exist. The buildings are empty, and grass and weeds grow where hundreds of people once hurried along busy streets. Many ghost towns are now historical sites, where people can see how a boomtown of the Old West looked over 100 years ago.

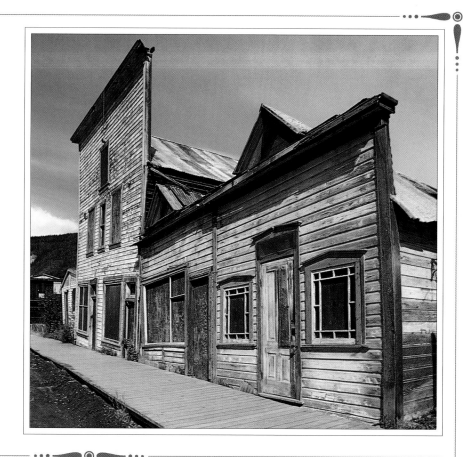

The Klondike gold rush ended almost as quickly as it began. People moved away and left buildings like these empty.

GLOSSARY

claim A piece of land chosen by a miner on which he or she searched for gold

claim jumping Mining on a piece of land that was claimed by another miner

commissioner's office The office at which prospectors paid for and registered their claims so others could not claim the same land

deposit An amount of material that builds up naturally

flogging A severe punishment that involves being lashed with a leather strap

lode A deposit of gold or other metals

malnutrition Sickness caused by lack of healthy food or starvation

migration The act of moving to a different place to live

placer gold Deposits of gold found in riverbeds and shallow underground areas

reservation An area of land set aside by the government on which Native Americans live

scow A flat-bottomed boat or raft which miners used to carry equipment over a river

tent stores Temporary stores made of tents that were moved from place to place for the purpose of selling food and tools to miners

tramway A system of overhead wires that is powered by an engine and pulls heavy loads up a steep hill

vein deposits Quantities of gold that lie underground in strips between layers of rock

wagon trains Groups of covered wagons in which many settlers traveled to the West

washing (gold) The process of using water to separate gold from dirt and gravel

vigilantes People who take the law into their own hands by punishing others

INDEX

African Americans 16

boomtowns 22-23, 26, 31

buffalo 20, 21

businesses 6, 8, 14, 19, 22, 23, 27, 30

California 6, 7, 8, 9, 16, 21, 24, 25, 29, 30

Canada 4, 6, 7, 25

children 18-19, 21

Chilkoot Pass 28

claims 5, 10, 11, 13, 16, 18, 19, 20, 21, 23, 24, 27, 29

crime 24, 25, 28

dangers 8, 9, 27-28

Dawson City 6, 7, 8, 23

equipment 7, 14, 21, 27, 30

Europe 4, 16

families 6, 8, 16, 18, 19, 26

food 7, 8, 9, 17, 18, 21, 27, 29

fool's gold 27

ghost towns 31

homes 8, 19, 21, 22, 26

jobs 18, 23

Klondike 7, 8, 9, 11, 17, 21, 23, 25, 28, 29, 30, 31

laws 24, 25

Marshall, James 6

Mexico 16

miners 5, 6, 7, 8, 9, 10, 11, 13, 14, 15, 16, 17, 18, 21, 22, 23, 24, 25, 27, 28, 29

money 14, 17, 18, 19, 22, 23, 27, 30

mountains 4, 7, 9, 28

Native Americans 20-21, 30

panning 13, 14, 23

police 24, 25

prospectors *see* miners

rivers 5, 6, 7, 8, 9, 11, 13, 21, 23, 28, 30

San Francisco 6, 8, 16, 23, 30

school 19

settlers 9, 21, 27, 30

sickness 9, 21, 25, 28, 29

stores 14, 19

tools 8, 10, 13, 14-15, 16

towns 4, 6, 18, 22, 23, 26, 29, 30, 31

travel 4, 5, 6, 8, 9, 18, 27, 28, 30

United States 4, 6

vigilantes 24, 25

wagons 9, 22, 28

women 11, 17, 18-19

ACKNOWLEDGMENTS

Photographs and reproductions
The Bancroft Library, University of California, Berkeley: pages 6, 8 (bottom), 15, 16 (top), 23 (bottom); California State Parks: pages 16 (left and bottom), 17 (bottom), 18, 27 (bottom); Dawson City Museum and Historical Society: pages 7, 11, 17 (top both), 21, 23 (top); Mark Horn: page 9; George H.H. Huey: page 26; *Walking Coyote and the Buffalo Orphans* ©1982 Tom Lovell, The Greenwich Workshop®, Inc. (detail): page 20; Clark James Mishler: pages 12, 27 (top), 29, 31; National Museum of American Art, Washington DC / Art Resource, NY (detail): pages 10-11; Charles M. Russell, *The Whiskey Smugglers*, National Cowboy Hall of Fame, Oklahoma City (detail): page 25; Special Collections, University of Washington Libraries, Hegg: pages 17 (middle right) (#555), 19 (#458), 28 (top) (#2164), 28 (bottom) (#106); other images by Image Club Graphics and Digital Stock

Illustrations and colorizations
Barbara Bedell: pages 13, 14-15, 29
Bonna Rouse: title page, pages 4-5, 6, 8 (map), 22

1 2 3 4 5 6 7 8 9 0   Printed in the U.S.A.   8 7 6 5 4 3 2 1 0 9